Business Pearls

Business and Life Quotes

By Sharon Mclean

Business Pearls

Published by Business With Excellence (BWE Publishing)

PO Box 2501

Coulsdon

Surrey

CR5 3YA

www.businesswithexcellence.com

info@businesswithexcellence.com

ISBN-13: 978-0-9927360-0-2

Endorsements

Sharon is a very generous entrepreneur not only to her colleagues but her industry peers. I have had the pleasure to collaborate on a number of projects with Sharon and you will always be guaranteed to have the highest quality delivery, up to date information and more importantly a delightful personality. Sharon comes highly recommended.

Sonia Brown MBE, Founder & Director NBWN

Business With Excellence events are a good opportunity to be inspired, learn practical tips to improve your business and build up your network. Sharon communicates key concepts and strategies clearly. These might include: Who is your market? How to get more customers or best practice for some area of the day-to-day running of your business. You always leave an event with an idea of how to improve your business. Business With Excellence events encourage attendees to gage areas of your business that can improve and get you to explore how to broaden your business scope.

Sheila Marshall, Business Owner, Aniku LTD

The 1-2-1 mentoring session I had with Sharon was great, she opened my eyes to things I did not see and gave me some nuggets which is now moving my business forward. Also, I love to attend her networking events as they are very productive and empowering.

Joe Oluwa, Peak Performance Coach

I have worked with Sharon both during my time at Business Link and recently in my role at Free Agent. Sharon is an inspiring person with bags of enthusiasm and is always looking to help and support small business owners achieve their goals. I would highly recommend her if you are looking for a delivery partner to work with or if you are seeking support in growing your business.

Matthew Perkins, Head of SME Engagement

Sharon is a meticulous Business Woman who's specialism in Marketing & Networking is second-to-none!...Straight-forward, on-point Marketing information that actually produces results. She's a 'No-gimmicks' Marketing & Networking specialist that taught me a lot about Marketing my Invention. I've met many 'Marketeers'...but none like this fine young Lady! Give her a try and see for yourself.

Donna Copeland, Inventor, DIVANI Designs

Sharon is an inspirational lady with a strong work ethic and is a real encouragement to people wanting to start a business or who are in business. The success stories speak for themselves. Sharon is not someone who speaks out of book knowledge but out of personal experience and from a position of personal success in her field. I would have no hesitation in recommending Sharon (indeed, I do!) to anyone looking for a business mentor or adviser. I count it a privilege to be associated with Sharon.

Jan Owbridge, EVP Genistar

Sharon is a tireless entrepreneur and manager who has, through her constant focus on her customers' needs, developed a vast network of clients, repeat customers and contacts. She is stupendously well organised, consistent, and provides a very professional service.

Adrian Ashe, Head of Programme Management Office, NHS WLCCG

Dedication

I dedicate this book to every person who has a
business idea in their head, those who have just started their
business and those who seek to grow their current business.
It is my intention to provide you with the wisdom you need to
use your gifts and talents to be successful in business
through your entrepreneurship and dedication to your dream.

Acknowledgement

Business is progressive and I have been blessed to have a range of people throughout my life who have supported me in my endeavours. I would like to acknowledge my parents, Herbert and Miriam Lawrence who provided the emotional stability in my formative years and the exposure to my first taste of entrepreneurship. In addition, I would like to recognise the value of my personal family; my husband Noel and my children who have afforded me the understanding and time to be a successful business woman and those in business who unknowingly inspired me at crucial times in my development.

Contents

Why Business Pearls?

 Pearls are of great worth and are formed in an oyster shell when an intruder such as a grain of sand or a bit of floating food slips in between one of the two shells of the oyster.

To protect itself from irritation the oyster will quickly begin covering the uninvited visitor with layers and layers of nacre. This is how the gem is formed. It is a miraculous event.

Business pearls are quotes and memoirs of wisdom that are designed to keep you moving forward in business. All the quotes and memoirs are born out of my business journey that started in 2002 of challenges and success.

These quotes have been an inspiration to me and has helped me to keep me focused on my business and will hopefully do the same for you. As you apply these pearls of wisdom to your business and share it with others, you will continue to grow far beyond the intrusions that may come into your business. I trust you will continue to find these quotes and memoirs rare, fine, admirable and valuable to you just like pearls. This book can be used by those who are new to business, individual business owners, personnel within companies, trainers, consultants and business coaches, in order to empower their learners, students and clients. Words seem to have the power to live well beyond our years.

In recent years, some explorers found the wreckage of a ship that had been at the depths of the sea for approximately 400 years. Amazingly they found pearls intact! I hope that these 'business pearls' will provide a lifetime of wisdom for you in business, regardless of the challenges that lie ahead.

Enjoy!

Sharon Mclean

Pearls for Starting

~ Pearl 1 ~

"You don't get to choose when you are born or when you die but you can choose what you do in between."

Every person who has been born comes with their own DNA and personality trait. You are made the way you are for a reason.

Circumstances of life can sometimes seek to define the type of person you become. This could include your upbringing, challenges you may have encountered, friendships and opportunities that may have become available to you. Good choices will invariably bring fulfilment and lead you into becoming who you were meant to be; the best you!

After years of trying out different types of businesses and being encouraged by others to go into partnership with them, I decided to choose what I was passionate about and use my gifts, skills and abilities to make a difference.

Action Point:

List your gifts, which are generally, the things that you are naturally good at. List your skills, which can include qualifications and competencies you have acquired through training and education. Consider how you can utilise what you have been given your current time and resources.

~ Pearl 2 ~

"Your mind is an incredibly complex organ: use it to your advantage."

As a counsellor, I have dealt with a range of different people who have had varying degrees of challenge in relation to their mental health. One thing has become abundantly clear; our mind controls so many things. The mind is able to go into the past, present and future as well as causing our bodies and emotions to react in certain ways. Many people say 'you are what you think' and there is some truth in that.

When I first started Business With Excellence, I had the belief that I could be successful. I then went and put my thoughts into action by contacting organisations that I could work and partner with. There was rejection along the way. I used my mind to my advantage by maintaining a mindset that said, "**with all the no's eventually someone would say yes**" and they did!

My first funding to run a business community project came after asking 10 times! I used my mind to maintain belief and regulate my responses.

Action Point:

What do you believe about yourself and your business? Develop a positive mentality and then remain resilient until you see things change.

~ Pearl 3~

"We all get the same amount of time during the day, some use it some waste it. What do you do?"

What do you do in a day? You can plan your most productive time around when you are at your best and most alert. Consider whether you are a morning or evening person and split your activities into morning, afternoon and evening. Are you procrastinating and wasting time on things you find no motivation to progress?

Interestingly, the word 'procrastination', is made up of two Latin words, *pro* which means 'for' and *crastinus* which means tomorrow. Tomorrow is always a day away. Take advantage of opportunities on the day they are presented to you. You can use your time to do something new the next day.

Action Point:

Choose the time of day when you are most productive and do those things first. You will feel more fulfilled. Prioritise your time in relation to the structure of the goals you set for yourself.

~ Pearl 4 ~

"Think, decide then act."

This is a good procedure to follow when wanting to start a business or introduce a new product or service.

Thinking involves going through in your mind all the different scenarios, the advantages, disadvantages, the timings and costings.

There are many things to think about regarding business but it is important to have some sort of template to check against. Decisions are crucial. There comes a point where you have to make a decision and commit to it.

The last course of action, which helps to put your thought process into reality, is by doing something tangible.

How many thoughts are still in your mind that has not been actioned?

Action Point:

Take a day out of your regular schedule and find a place where you will not be interrupted in order to think, decide and act. If you want to expedite the process, then it is useful to have a mentor you can work alongside to ensure your decisions are informed and wise.

~ Pearl 5 ~

"Structure is the key to things lasting in your life. Examine your structure."

Structure is important in business as it gives a model for you to operate within. Customers are the lifeblood of any business. Do you have structures to engage with existing customers and gain new ones on a regular basis?

I remember making the mistake of relying heavily on one client for my income due to them purchasing many of my products and services. As their needs changed they no longer required many of my services. This experience taught me to put a structure in place to continually look after my existing clients and also look for new clients on a consistent basis. Good business structures create reviews and contingencies.

Have you examined your marketing, financial, operational and legal structures for your business? It is good to have a regular review to see if anything has changed.

Action Point:

Think about your structure and choose one you would like to put in place now. After you have completed it, go onto the next one so you have all your structures in place.

~ Pearl 6 ~

"Sharpen your skills you can get more done in less time."

I t is important not to take your skills for granted. There is tremendous competition in business and standards are improving, therefore it is important that you improve your skills. List the skills you need to do your business effectively and consider whether they are progressing, static or declining.

In recent years, I realised that I needed to update my computer skills. I spent years writing most of my ideas, customer details and accounts on paper but realised time could be saved by having files on the computer which could be updated more easily. This will free up time for you to concentrate on the important aspects of your business.

Take time to sharpen your skills through going on courses and engaging in self directed learning.

Action Point:

List the skills you need to sharpen and research opportunities for you to improve them.

~ Pearl 7 ~

"Improve where you are now. Take steps to grow."

love to set goals of what I want to achieve in the short, medium and long term. This can be done over 1 year, 3 years or over 5 years or more. Look at where you are now in business and plan to make consistent steps to grow. This is more manageable than taking giant leaps that can at times, bring you into areas of incompetence.

An example, of improving where you are now, might mean investing in a particular piece of equipment for your business and then learning how to use it effectively in order to improve the way in which you do business or communicate with your customers. It could also be enlarging your customer database or taking on additional staff.

Action Point:

When starting something new, take gradual steps in order to feel comfortable and build confidence. Write out your goals and have them somewhere visible so you can refer to them from time to time. Adjust your daily routine to match your goals.

Pearls for Growing

~ Pearl 8 ~

"When you are prepared, more doors will open."

Working with a range of businesses in the creative, retail and service industry has taught me about the value of process and preparation. The dedication to detail by some of my clients to make a handbag or to create a bespoke cake confirmed to me the need to do business with excellence but also to believe that excellence and preparation will eventually open more doors for business.

To deliver a cake may take one hour depending on the destination and to run a day's training course may be a maximum of 7 hours. Imagine if the preparation was not done, delivering a cake that is of poor quality would have wasted your journey and having people attend training courses where you were not prepared, will create dissatisfied customers.

I recall taking a whole day out to rearrange my presentation to a small group of business people. I prepared a range of activities that could be done in groups and individually.

To my surprise when I arrived at the venue there were over 300 delegates waiting. I was shocked to say the least but I was prepared. The amount of people that turned up was secondary to the prepared content I had. I was thankful

I was prepared and as a result, I was able to secure more work from other business people who wanted a follow up session.

Action Point:

Prepare yourself and through practice, develop competence on your own before you work with others. Ensure that what you offer is of value and your resources are ready for public use. It is better to postpone an engagement than to be unprepared for that engagement.

~ Pearl 9 ~

"You were created with at least one creative gift. Use it!"

Creativity is inside us all. It may be in creative thinking or action. I would love to be able to make things with my hands but my creative gift is in my thinking.

I love to use it to think up exciting and innovative programmes for my clients. Creativity will challenge you to 'think outside the box.'

Studies show we only use 11% of our brain. What steps are you taking to use more of the 89%?

Action Point:

Are you creative in thinking or action? Write down one creative gift that you have and start using it. List the ways you can do this.

~ Pearl 10 ~

"If you are not improving you are falling behind."

t is so easy to become stuck in our ways and continue to do what we know and are comfortable with. Our world is constantly changing. In recent years, we have seen high street businesses, which were once market leaders, no longer trading, due to a change in consumer habits and social trends.

Action Point:

What do you need to update or improve about your business? Be honest. You can do this by self evaluation, asking your customers or researching your industry to see what are the latest trends. This will help you to keep up-to-date.

~ Pearl 11 ~

"Produce more in response to demand."

When I first started Business With Excellence I only offered seminars on a Saturday every week. I realised my customers wanted more.

Every service I now offer is as a result of my customers feedback; what a privileged position to be in! You can produce more by predicting future demand or by asking your current or potential customers what they need.

Action point:

Ask your customers what other products or services they would need and produce it to suits their needs and wants.

~ Pearl 12 ~

"Treasure skills and talent."

As human beings it is common for us to think the things we can do are 'no big deal'. This was pointed out to me by my customers when I would organise one event after another without any headache. It was not until I started speaking to other business owners who struggled with this that I realised that this was a talent I had.

Action Point:

What are you doing well in your business? Treasure it and do not take it for granted. Are you currently doing something for free that others would actually pay for?

~ Pearl 13 ~

"Solution orientated people are invaluable to life and business. What problems are you providing solutions for?"

People love to find solutions to their problems and situations. One way of looking at business is to see business as a problem solving enterprise. The more problems your business solves, the more valuable your business will be.

Action Point:

Ask your potential and current customers what their concerns are and look to provide the solution. It is a 'win win' situation for business. Write down the biggest problem your business could solve.

~ Pearl 14 ~

"The world is changing fast are you continually moving?"

t is important to keep up-to-date with what is going on around you. Many business owners make the mistake of moving fast with every phase.

Some trends are seasonal but it is important you remain relevant. As long as you are moving you can go at a pace that is comfortable for you.

Action Point:

Be aware of the pace you have set. Is it too fast, too slow or just right for you?

Pearls for Engaging With Customers

~ Pearl 15 ~

"Take advantage of the time you are using."

I often hear small business owners say they do not have time to focus on the most important aspects of their business due to the challenges of managing all aspects of their business and personal life.

You can maximise your time by using your available time in a more productive way. More time does not necessarily mean better time. Ignore distractions that will compete for your time. Time remains a precious commodity.

Action Point:

Look at the available and quality time you have in a day for your business. Set a time clock. If you have an hour, use that time effectively. It may mean ignoring any other distractions that may want to compete for your time such as the mobile phone, emails, friends, housework, and social media. Do one thing at a time.

~ Pearl 16 ~

"Associate with people who inspire you and challenge you."

We are all created as relational beings. Generally, we are either an introvert or an extrovert. There is only so much we can do effectively on our own.

Having people around us who inspire us and who challenge us will have a positive impact on our business.

Action Point:

Who are the key people in your life? Who inspires you? Who are the key people that you admire in business who are much further than you? List your business influencers.

~ Pearl 17 ~

"If you are on the right track keep moving."

I f you decided to go to Birmingham and realised you were on your way to London, you would conclude that you were moving but moving in the wrong direction.

Sometimes at the start of your business or when you are in the growing stage, it is easy to think that things are not going as quickly as you want and it is easy to go in another direction.

In my early years of business I wanted more income so would take on additional opportunities to make money for the sake of it. I then realised that it took me in a completely different direction to the one I had originally intended. I had to go back to the core reason I entered business and this helped me to stay on the right track.

Action Point:

Write down the "why" or the reason you have set up in business and stay on track. Be true to your vision. List any areas you feel you may have deviated from your core reason for going into business.

~ Pearl 18 ~

"Great leaders are ordinary people who walk in front."

The advantage of running your own business is that you get an opportunity to lead from the front. You are not reliant on anyone, neither are you responsible for other people's actions.

As a business owner I realised I still have other things in my life to deal with such as family, health and dealing with the day to day challenges of life.

These are things that ordinary people go through every day. The big difference is that as a business owner leading your business, you have to walk in front by starting things. You are the initiator and carrier of your business. It takes courage and wisdom. It is not enough to be courageous in business; you also need to lead with wisdom.

Action Point:

Think about how you are leading yourself. What things do you need to start now? Consider how you can lead more effectively.

~ Pearl 19 ~

"The higher you climb the easier it is to see the overall picture."

Sometimes when running a business it is easy to look at things from your own viewpoint or in the confines of your own space which is the here and now.

I run regular business retreats to encourage business owners to work on their businesses rather than in their businesses.

By taking time out to work on your business you can look at things from a different perspective. I call it the 'bird's eye' view. To have a bird's eye view it is important to move to a different place and see things differently.

Action Point:

Take time out for a few hours or a day and look at your business from a different angle. Is it going in the direction that you expected? Are you making money?

~ Pearl 20 ~

"Focus on doing one thing at a time."

This is my favourite quote. It reaps huge rewards. It is so easy to try and do many things at the same time. In most cases in business, it does not work. Juggling is a great skill but the risk of dropping something is high! When I juggled too many things, I invariably started many things but did not complete them.

By having your focus on one thing there is a sense of accomplishment when you have completed it.

Action Point:

Write down one thing that you would like to complete. Only cross it off when you have done it and then write down the next thing and repeat the same exercise. This will give you clarity of thinking in your business.

~ Pearl 21 ~

"Everything starts in seed form."

There is a natural progression of growth that manifests as a result of your daily business routine. Whether you are at a pre-start up business phase or growing your current business, everyone has to make a start. The start can be in thought, action or on paper.

Once you have made a start on something the secret is to keep going on a regular basis. If you have one customer, keep serving them until you get your next customer.

Action Point:

What seeds can you sow today that will reap a harvest in the future?

Pearls for Remaining Positive

~ Pearl 22 ~

"Let others recognise your growth not you."

Growth is not easily recognised by a business owner. We can become so engrossed in growing our business that we can fail to identify the small areas we have progressed in. It is good practice to gain an objective and fresh perspective on your business, often from someone you do not work with or someone who has been exposed to your business for some time.

Action Point:

Speak to colleagues and customers who have used your products or services over a period of time and let them comment on your growth. You may be pleasantly surprised and could be spurred on to do other things.

~ Pearl 23 ~

"Everyday is a new day, your chance to start again."

We all get the same amount of time given to us within a day. What we do with our day is our choice.

There has been times when my day has not gone the way I planned it. Be optimistic and realise you can start again. If a business idea fails, use the experience to start a new one!

Action Point:

What fresh and new opportunities have been presented to you today? Seize the moment!

~ Pearl 24 ~

"Whatever you practice you become good at."

Don't be afraid of testing something before you go public. Practice speaking to customers by perhaps recording yourself in mock consultations or writing bids that you can send to friends and gain feedback. There is a saying that 'practice makes perfect'.

Each day we practice out skills by serving our customers but we can also perfect our skills by having a season of observing the way others in business interact with their customers.

Action Point:

Consider ways through which you can practice your approaches to and methods in business. Consider shadowing someone who is experienced in business in order to learn more methods.

~ Pearl 25 ~

"Everything has a beginning, make a start."

So many times in business I have thought about offering a new service and kept the thought in my head. It was not until I put pen to paper and started that I realised I could put a start date to what I had done.

Start dates are important but must be realistic. Start dates help to create excitement and gives you the opportunities to build momentum.

Action Point:

Set a start date for your business or new business initiative. List key actions that can create momentum towards the start date.

~ Pearl 26 ~

"The problems that matter to you, are the problems you can probably solve."

Problems are there to be solved but you cannot solve every problem. What concerns do you have and what are you passionate about solving? This could be your answer to your next business or additional product or service.

I discovered a problem early on that so many professional women who took a break from work to have children, were battling with the decision to either go back to work and make money or to stay at home with their children.

I could see some wanted to do both. When Business With Excellence was launched, we worked with these women at unconventional business times such as evenings and weekends, in order to help them come to their own decisions. Some chose reduced hours, other chose flexible working and some followed their passion by transferring their existing skills into setting up a business.

Action Point:

Think of the problems you encounter but list the ones that challenge you and inspire you to find a solution. Consider the solutions and be the solution.

~ Pearl 27 ~

"Money is a small ingredient that needs to be mixed with other aspects of business."

There are many things that go into the mix to make a business successful. If there is money and no passion, the business activities will be limited.

Money in business goes well, when it is mixed with other things. The main ingredients I have used in my business over time are passion, commitment, determination, planning, listening to my customers' wants and needs and risk taking.

When Business With Excellence first started I mixed some of these 'ingredients' with as little as £100 and was able to negotiate and secure community premises for me to rent in order to run my courses.

Action Point:

Write down all the key ingredients/ character traits that you feel you need to run your business and then add the small ingredient of money to it.

~ Pearl 28 ~

"Stability enables you to work from a secure base."

F eeling stable is important in running a business. Stability means different things to different people. Stability for me means having a designated space to work from as well as having a consistent flow of customers to work with.

This has been built up over a period of time. It is from this base that I have felt comfortable to introduce new things and take on additional responsibilities.

Action Point:

Think about what stability means to you and work on becoming more stable.

Pearls for Innovation

~ Pearl 29 ~

"Things change, people change, keep with it; that is customer service."

We are constantly changing and evolving. You may not have a customer for life anymore. The best advice I can give when running a business is to keep in touch with the changes that your customers are communicating to you regarding your business.

I am pleased to say that every service or product that I provide is a result of my customers changing needs.

One example of this is the Skype mentoring service. This enables customers who are in far geographic locations to still benefit and connect with the business.

This service is not something I would have chosen automatically, it came as a result of listening. Do your customers think you are charging too much? Customer service in its simplest form is about serving your customer.

Action Point:

Devise a short questionnaire asking your customers what their current needs are? Assess and review the way your customers might be behaving and note changes in how they access your services or note those who no longer do.

~ Pearl 30 ~

"Relationships can propel you forward or hold you back. Choose wisely."

C hoice is a powerful gift we all have. In business I have come across all types of relationships. There are those who are working and associating with you only to get the best they can get out of the relationship.

There are others who see it both ways as giving and receiving. I have had experience of both in my business. The relationships where some business owners have only connected with me for personal and not mutual benefits, has at times, left me feeling used and unproductive.

However, other business relationships where there has been giving and receiving, has helped me to focus and work to my strengths and also helped me to appreciate and promote the other persons attributes.

Action Point:

Think about the types of relationships you have in business at the moment and decide which ones are right for you and make the changes to help you propel forward.

~ Pearl 31 ~

"The gift of an individual impresses others immediately but the character of a person outlasts over time."

This statement, throughout my years in business, has been a reality. Upon meeting people for the first time, most have been impressed with my knowledge of and innovation in business. However, I realised that what has kept me going is my character; perseverance, courage and integrity.

I like to see my client relationships as long term, so I treat them in a way that encourages longevity.

Action Point:

List your character traits and aim to see them working each day in your business.

~ Pearl 32 ~

"Sometimes opportunities comes from places and people you would least expect seize, the moment."

Everyday you wake up there are new opportunities. Early in my business journey, I had the experience of a contract being taken away from me due to lack of funding. My first response was to panic. However, I began to market my products and services in other areas, building relationships with people and just talking casually about what I do.

As a result, I was presented with an opportunity to offer business support in an area I would have never chosen. I saw the opportunity, seized the moment and I am still benefiting from it today.

My learners have experienced this too. After teaching a course in a local library, one of the staff came over to give feedback on their work.

As a result of talking to the staff, I was able to share their experience of what they do and was able to pass on a referral to the learner. We would not have known this unless a conversation started.

Action Point:

Listen to your customers, competitors and business associates and watch out for new opportunities. Use conversations to open up fresh opportunities.

~ Pearl 33 ~

"Be prepared for the expected and unexpected customer?"

Preparation time is never lost time. I spend hours preparing my courses to benefit the different types of people who will attend. On one occasion, I was very upset as attendee's cancelled at the last minute.

My thought was I spent all that time preparing a presentation to go through with them. However, I was surprised to see another client turn up and was overjoyed with the step by step guide I produced for others. This attendee felt that the guide was 'written especially' for them.

In your business always get ready and use the time on your own to practice going through things to feel more confident. It is an art. The more you practice the better you will be.

Action Point:

Choose something you would like to present to your customer and practice it.

~ Pearl 34 ~

"3 ways to deal with change ignore it, resist it, or adapt to it."

This is crucial in business. Throughout my time in business, I have seen some businesses flourish and others just stop. Upon closer analysis, I came to the conclusion that their demise had been down to their inability to adapt to change.

There are many changes you have to encounter in business. Some of the changes I have experienced were changes in consumer taste, increasing competition, government changes and changes in technology. If you ignore change, things will pass you by. If you resist it, sometimes you can feel overwhelmed but if you adapt to it, you can flow with the change and be open to new ideas for your business.

Action Point:

What changes in your business are you ignoring or resisting? Make a decision to adapt to it.

~ Pearl 35 ~

"Serve others well and you will have a continual service, produce products well and you will increase your productivity."

Service is about meeting your customer's needs but it is also about treating them well. Just by asking a customer how they are can represent to them that you care about their well-being and value them.

When customers see you adapt your products and respond to their needs they will develop a sense of loyalty to you. The following is an example of how this strategy worked in my business. I had customers complaining that the location of my training courses were too far for them to travel to.

As a result, I now do an event in a central location, so it is easier for many of my customers to attend. I have also offered training on Skype for customers who live in others parts of the world.

Action Point:

What is the best you can do for your customer? What products can you produce in response to your client's requests?

Pearls for Authenticity

~ Pearl 36 ~

"Use your individuality to enhance your diversity."

Were all born with unique gifts and talents.
One of the first exercises I do on my
business start up course is to ask people
what their unique selling point is.

I get them to write down all the things that they believe
they are good at. Some find it easy others find it hard. When
you sit down and begin to self assess, you will often find that
there are things you do in a special way that is unique to
you.

Once you have found this out, use it in your
promotional business literature. Although someone may be
in a similar profession to you they are not you.

Action Point:

Talk about who you are, what you do and what you are
passionate about to potential customers and gauge their
interest. Discover how unique what you do might be!

~ Pearl 37 ~

"If you are not happy in what you are doing, change it."

The power to change things, are in your hands, regarding your skills and productivity in business.

When I first started in business I was not happy that I was giving away good quality business advice for literally next to nothing. I got very upset about this and then I realised that most people were only taking advantage because I allowed it.

When I decided to make a change I lost some of my customers but kept the ones who appreciated the service. Consequently, I was able to work with them on a more consistent basis and felt happy doing so. The relationship was then mutually beneficial.

When you change things you are not happy with, you feel fulfilled and have that greater sense of achievement. Try it and see.

Action Point:

Write down the list of things that you are not happy with in your business and then come up with a solution of how you are going to change it.

~ Pearl 38~

"Space is an environment for creativity to flow. Find your own space."

We all have creativity within us. It may be a creative mind or a creative hand. My biggest inspiration for new ideas has come when I am out on my own with a clear head in a clear environment surrounded by lots of space normally a large park or garden.

Action Point:

Choose your favourite place to relax and unwind. Stay there for a while and watch your creativity flow. You will actually achieve more with your time when you identify a creative place.

~ Pearl 39 ~

"Dreams can become reality through action."

I started my business with an initial thought, dreaming about how I wanted to work with different types of people to help them put their business ideas into some sort of structure that would give them an income as a living.

It was not until I took my first step of booking a community centre to run a seminar that it became a reality. My actions brought my thoughts to life.

As long as it stayed in my head it was a dream, as soon as I did something about it, then it became a reality.

Action Point:

What action do you need to take to let your dreams become a reality? Write them down and then start doing something constructive to fulfil each one. Keep a check list of start and completion dates.

~ Pearl 40 ~

"There is a phrase called 'I can't' and 'I can.' Choose which one you will use."

Thimes all comes down to choice. In the early years of my business I would write everything down on paper which is how I would get my thoughts out.

A few of my colleagues later suggested that I should start using the computer more for emails, newsletters and then introduced me to social media. My first thought was I can't do this as I did not have the skills.

Once I weighed up the benefits it would bring to my business, I chose to learn how to do it. It is reaping huge rewards now.

Action Point:

What are some of the things you have said you can't do? Find a way to get support or outsource the work to others.

~ Pearl 41 ~

"Innovation will cause you to continually stay in business."

Y ou can do the same thing but in a different way. Adjusting the presentation, method and structure of a service can lead to a new niche of customers.

Action Point:

List out all the products and services you want to provide or currently provide and offer them in a different way.

~ Pearl 42 ~

"Relate at three levels someone who can support you, someone you can support and someone you can walk along side, then you will have a mentor, be a mentee and a peer."

Having these three levels of relationships keeps you balanced in business and doesn't allow you to neglect your personal needs. It also gives you the opportunity to be mentored and to mentor others and have a peer relationship.

Multi-level relationships are important in business. Relate with someone who can support what you do, relate with someone you can support in what they do and relate with someone who can support you as a person.

Action Point:

Write down at least two names from each level and work on those relationships. It will add strength to your business and you will feel fulfilled.

Reflection Exercises

Inspiration

Where does your inspiration come from? Find time and space to know. Is it from people, creation or things? Once you have found out, utilise that source in order to receive new insight. I get my inspiration from being around people. I take on new challenges, set new goals and continually dream big without limits. True inspiration impacts the mind and soul in a way that instigates a passionate response.

Knowledge

What knowledge do you possess, that you can impart to others, in order to simplify their life and business? Are you packaging your knowledge into products and services to share with others? If not, why? Begin to attribute value to the knowledge you have.

The person you are

Who are you? Do you know your maximum potential and your gifts, skills and abilities? It is who you are that makes you unique and authentic. Are your priorities right? How much time and money would you put into developing yourself as opposed to having flashy brochures and a modern website? Whilst these externals items can in some ways affect the way people perceive you, your personal development must be paramount. Self investment is the most important cost you can bring into your business as when you are mentally and professionally healthy, that is when you are in your strongest position to sustain growth in your business.

There is always a room with a view

Take time and space to go into a 'room' with a view. Many hotels cost their rooms based on the quality of the view from the window. A room with a view gives you the opportunity to see beyond where you are situated and see outside the 'room'. You will see things outside from different levels and appreciate the scenery. Take time out to look at your business from different angles. Visit other people's business meetings other than your own. Read different articles from personnel who have alternative ways to do business. Appreciate where you are now but start to 'see' where you potentially can reach.

Authenticity and uniqueness

There is only one you and many similar businesses to yours. Create authenticity and uniqueness by focusing on your strengths in business and communicate that in the most effective way that will support the needs and wants of your customers and on a regular basis. Be creative and be the best you that you can be. What are your gifts, talents and abilities (G.T.A)? Make a list of them, write them down and most of all use them in your business. You may be pleasantly surprised to discover the reason why your customers keep coming back is due to your G.T.A.

The power of brainstorming

Our minds are very powerful and productive. It is amazing how many thoughts go through our mind on a daily basis. What if you shared your thoughts and ideas with likeminded people? Brainstorming is very effective when your thoughts become words and your words then become action points. Brainstorming is one of the activities where goals and dreams begin to build momentum.

Targeting customers

Customers are everywhere. The first step is to write out a list of your products and services and then break down in detail the type of person who would buy these products and services on a regular basis. Through this process, you will often find that certain types of customers fall into multiple segments and others are very specific. This exercise has to be continued all the way through the life of your business to keep your customers buying from you. Once you have defined your target group you can look for them in a range of places. Successful business owners will always be clear on who their target group is. Once you have found your target group you can then decide the best way to get your message to them.

The purpose of money in business

Money is an essential element in business; the following are some key reasons why.

- It is useful for starting and growing your business
- It can be used as your main income for living
- It can be used to develop a community
- It keeps the economy going

Be mindful of how money is working for you in your business. Do you have the right amount of customers to get going in business? Have you priced your products and services correctly? Do you know how much profit you are making? Do you have a short, medium and long term financial goal for your business? These questions are important for you to answer so you know where you stand regarding money in your business.

The Importance of longevity

When starting a business have in mind it is a marathon and not a sprint. This will take the pressure off you to do everything straight away which is impossible. Pace yourself one step or one goal at a time. Complete the goal or step before moving onto the next.

It is always an honour to see businesses that are still running over a long period of time despite outside challenges such as the recession or other internal factors. Customers will develop trust because of your longevity.

Confidence

Confidence is essential in your business. You have to wear it like a badge. Carry it with you wherever you go. Your confidence can be developed in the following ways. Practice the art of presenting your product and services to as many potential customers as possible. Gain knowledge and up- to-date information in your area of expertise.

Trust your own judgement. Continue to build your confidence internally and externally. Believe in yourself, your gifts, skills and abilities. Work towards your strengths and communicate that to others. Associate with like-minded people who will inspire, support and challenge you. Follow your dreams and put them into action.

Operations

Have you considered how you would like your business to operate on a daily basis?

How many hours can you work? Where will you work from? Who will you work with?

These are decisions you will need to make before you start and they may change as your business grows, so it is important to review it on a regular basis. Consider the types of customers you would like to work with and build this up over time.

Consider having a V.I.P group of customers who you regularly work with. This will represent the best return on your marketing efforts. This is easy to identify. Who loves your products and services and will continually buy? Make your list, and approach them. A circle is something that goes round and round.

Keep a continuous circle of customers and introduce new ones into the circle all the time. This will keep your business going.

Systems

Systems are ways of doing things. It consists of mechanism and procedures and it is the hub of what makes things work.

Think of some effective systems you will need to put in place to make your business a success. An effective system is one that works all the time with different personnel and can carry on when you are not there. The key ones to consider are operational, financial, marketing, online and legal,

All of these systems have strengths and weaknesses. By way of example, a strong online system can allow you to advertise your services to potential customers, connect with current customers and generate an income irrespective of whether you are engaged in a business activity or not. I try to use a variety of systems in order to help me accommodate the other activities in my life.

Reflect and list the systems you currently use. Once written, consider how you could network with other business people and learn from their systems. The following are a summary of some key additional systems.

A **financial system** is having a procedure in place for how you will file your records. Will it be online, offline or a mixture of both? Consider your pricing strategy, review your suppliers. Be aware of your most profitable service or products on a regular basis.

Marketing is the lifeblood of your business. No customers, no business. Consider your marketing systems. A key question is, 'what works best for your customers'? Think of having a time plan of what you will do over a period of time to keep existing customers and attract new ones. Implement the marketing strategy over an agreed timeframe then be consistent. There is power in repetition. Not everyone will hear your message at the same time.

Online systems are a great opportunity to tap into new markets and maximise time.

The list is endless. It could include social media, different payment systems, and automation. A fundamental element of online systems must therefore be the ability for the system to work for you, your business and customers. By way of example, one of the online systems that have worked effectively for me is an online payment system. It means when I am having an event or offering a service; customers can book and pay any time of the day, in any country due to having a web-link. For customers who still like the personal touch, they can book over the phone and their booking details can be done online whilst talking to me.

Your **legal systems** are very important, as in every industry there will be rules and laws to work by. What systems will you put in place to make sure you are kept updated?

Irrespective of your great business idea and bulging projects, everything can be undermined by a lack of good governance or failure to comply with the law. One of the ways I remain legally updated, is to subscribe to industry journals and receive regular email industry updates. It is also useful to have a legal person in your network that you can go to in order to gain insight in changes in the business arena that will impact your current practice.

By way of example, if you are going to be dealing with employment, premises, land, contracts or any long term agreements it is advisable to seek legal advice before going into it. It can save you money in the long term. When signing contracts, it is essential not just to read the terms and conditions but also to understand the implications of these terms.

Other Services

By Sharon McLean

If you enjoyed reading this book and would like to work with Sharon to take your business to the next level get in touch. Sharon is also available for public speaking engagements, mentoring, seminars and courses and is able to host, organise and run regular networking events

- Email: info@businesswithexcellence.com
- Follow us on twitter: twitter.com/sharonbwe
- Like us on face book: facebook.com/BusinessWithExcellence
- LinkedIn: Sharon Mclean
- www.businesswithexcellence.com